D0846848

The Tao of Yao:
Wit and Wisdom from the
"Moving Great Wall" Yao Ming

by Douglas Choi

For Soren, who is only 2-foot-7

HOUSTON PUBLIC LIBRARY

R01229 98494

Copyright ©2003 Almond Tree Books LLC
All rights reserved.

Except for appropriate use in critical reviews
or works of scholarship, the reproduction
or use of this work in any form or by any
electronic, mechanical or other means
now known or hereafter invented, including
photocopying and recording, and in any
information storage and retrieval system,
including electronic transmission, is
forbidden without the written permission of
the publisher.

Excerpt in Introduction reprinted with
permission from the Houston Chronicle
Publishing Company.

The quotations in this book are reproduced
from interviews with and stories about
Yao Ming.

**A portion of the proceeds of this book will
be donated to charitable organizations.**

Library of Congress Catalog Card Number:
2003091260
International Standard Book Number (ISBN):
0-9729208-0-3

Design by Chris Pew
www.machtalchemy.com

Cover illustration by Jamison Hunt
www.crimsonghost.com

Almond Tree Books LLC
5727 South Prentice Street
Seattle, Washington 98178
www.almondtreebooks.com

Douglas Choi is a corporate attorney in
Seattle, Washington. He is not even sure if
his high school had a basketball team. He
would not have made it anyway.

Printed in Canada

CONTENTS

INTRODUCTION

Growing up in Canada, hockey was the only sport that mattered to me. My heroes were guys like Guy Lafleur, Ken Dryden and Larry Robinson — white guys, all of them, 'cause that's all there were. It wasn't until I began law school at the University of Michigan in the fall of 1994 that I really paid any attention to any other sports. That September, a group of five highly-touted high school basketball stars began their freshman year at Michigan at the same time I began my legal studies there. These prized recruits, which included current NBA fixtures Chris Webber, Jalen Rose and Juwan Howard, became known as the "Fab Five" and I got swept up in the fanfare surrounding their arrival on campus along with everyone else. While at Michigan, I also followed the exploits of such gridiron heroes as Tyrone Wheatley and Heisman Trophy winner-to-be Desmond Howard. I went on to follow the professional careers of many of these college standouts. Of course, none of these guys looked anything like me either. That's because I'm Asian American.

Very few Asian or Asian American athletes have ever played in the major professional sports leagues. Of these sports, by far, Asians have made their most significant impact on baseball in terms of number of players and performance on the field, most notably represented by the success of Hideo Nomo of the LA Dodgers and Seattle Mariners All-Star and Gold Glove outfielder Ichiro Suzuki. The NHL welcomed its first athlete of Asian descent in 1991, when Jim Paek began his career with the Pittsburgh Penguins where he played on two Stanley Cup championship-winning teams. Even the NFL has had its share of Asian American players over the past two decades, including the former St. Louis Cardinal and UCLA All-American kicker John Lee (drafted in the second round of the 1986 NFL Draft), former New England Patriots offensive lineman Eugene Chung, Pittsburgh Steelers receiver Hines Ward (whose mother is Korean), and Dat Nguyen who currently starts for the Dallas Cowboys at linebacker. But the NBA seemed until very recently to be a kind of last frontier for athletes of Asian descent. It is a league in which the height of the average player is six feet, seven inches tall. Asians are stereotyped for being short. Well, truth be told, I don't know any who are 6-foot-7. It seemed likelier that NASCAR would see a black driver on the Winston Cup circuit before the NBA would see its first baller of Asian descent. Then, in April 2001, 7-foot-1 Wang ZhiZhi from China made his debut for the Dallas Mavericks at center. Wang has since moved on to the Los Angeles Clippers and was joined last season (2001-2002) by Chinese national Mengke Bateer, currently with the San Antonio Spurs. However, neither Wang nor Bateer has yet to distinguish themselves by their play on the court.

Then came Yao.

Picked first in the 2002 NBA Draft by the Houston Rockets, the 7-foot-5-inch Shanghai native generated a lot of buzz just by virtue of being the number one pick in the draft. Many observers felt the Rockets were making a huge gamble to select the largely-untested Chinese giant with the first pick. In his much-anticipated NBA regular-season debut against Indiana on October 30, 2002, Yao was held scoreless in 11 minutes of playing time, missing his only field goal attempt. Over the course of his next six games, he averaged only five points and four rebounds per game. The doubters and "player-haters" began to surface in a scene reminiscent of what happened with Ichiro Suzuki, the first Asian position player to start for a major league baseball team. In April 2001, at the start of Ichiro's first season with the Mariners, former Cincinnati Reds pitcher Rob Dibble was so sure the Japanese all-everything player would prove to be a flop here in America that he announced on an ESPN radio show that if Ichiro won the batting title, he would tattoo the outfielder's number 51 on his butt and run around Times Square naked. After Ichiro finished the season winning the AL MVP and Rookie of the Year titles, and sporting the best batting average in the majors, Dibble ate crow and followed through with his run around Times Square. In a curious validation of Nietzsche's idea of eternal recurrence, Charles Barkley, whose mouth was already well-acquainted with his foot, unwittingly followed Dibble's lead in prognosticating the rookie season results for this latest Asian sports sensation — this . . . Yao Ming, who he claimed made "Shawn Bradley look like Bill Russell" — when he boldly announced that he would kiss the rear end of Kenny Smith, his co-analyst on TNT's NBA studio show, if Yao Ming was able to score as many as 19 points in any one game in his first season with the Rockets.

Three days later, on November 17, 2002, in an away game against the Los Angeles Lakers, Yao dropped 20 points and six boards on the defending NBA champions, shooting 9-for-9 from the field in just 23 minutes. The Lakers were without Shaquille O'Neal, who was nursing an old toe injury, so the highly-anticipated matchup between the two massive pivot men did not take place; nevertheless, Yao gave hoops fans their first course from his Shanghai banquet and sealed a comeuppance encounter between Charles Barkley's lips and the hind quarters of a donkey that Kenny Smith rented to stand in for him during Barkley's promised "ass-kissing." Then, two games later, in the first half of a loss to the league-leading Dallas Mavericks, Yao made like Tiger at the '97 Masters and brought his 'A' game, tossing in 21 points and snaring seven boards in just 15 first-half minutes. He finished the contest with a season-high 30 points and 16 rebounds in 33 minutes of play. He was 10-for-12 from the field that night and, including that game, had made 31 of his last 35 field goal attempts. After his next five games, in which he, alternately, struggled and excelled, Yao was set to start against San Antonio's "twin towers," seven-footers David Robinson and Tim Duncan. As he had against the Mavericks, Yao rose to the occasion — this time in a winning cause, finishing with 27 points and 18 rebounds.

From the next morning's *Houston Chronicle*:

"Most of his teammates were still giddy on the court when Yao Ming plopped himself on the bench as if he had done nothing special.

Yao had begun to take over, grabbing the tough rebounds and making the big free throws Tim Duncan of the Spurs could not. Then Yao went further. He took Steve Francis' missed shot and, with a precise and powerful punch, shoved it back down. With the Spurs reeling into a timeout, Yao returned to the bench, where Cuttino Mobley, Glen Rice and Maurice Taylor stepped back and stared in awe. It was as if they looked long enough, they would believe what they had seen.

'I hope,' Yao said of his wide-eyed teammates, 'they don't think I'm a monster.'

Too late. They do.

Someday, the Rockets knew, they would pit their latest center prodigy against Duncan and let Yao carry them where he could. Someday came Tuesday, and Yao took the Rockets to an impressive 89-75 win before 11,120 at Compaq Center.

But more than breaking the Spurs' four-game winning streak against them, stretching their home winning streak to five games or moving into second place in the Midwest Division, the Rockets announced Yao's arrival again with the latest and greatest game of the 17 he has played.

'The big man is here,' Rice said. 'He is for real.'"

Indeed. Yao Ming was already a sports icon of the highest order in China before he brought his skills to North America. A nation of 1.3 billion hangs its hopes on Yao's broad shoulders and watches his every move to see what he will accomplish playing among the greatest basketball players in the world. He is rapidly gaining the respect of his NBA peers. He has become a hero to Houston sports fans.

But he is also "representing" for every Asian American male who dutifully shuffled off to med school or law school and, thus, will never, except vicariously, have the thrill of knocking down a three from the corner of the Staples Center or jamming the ball without benefit of a chair.

Douglas Choi
Seattle, February 2003

Inside the NBA on TNT, November 14, 2002;
Houston Chronicle, December 4, 2002

BIOGRAPHICAL INFORMATION

PERSONAL TIMELINE

Birth   On September 12, 1980, Yao Ming is born in Shanghai, People's Republic of China (PRC). He is an only child. Yao's father, Yao Zhi Yuan, stands 6-foot-7 and played center for both the Chinese national men's team and the Shanghai local team. His mother, Fang Feng Di, is 6-foot-3 and was a captain and center for China's national women's team.

Age 4   Begins paying adult bus fares on the public buses in Shanghai because of his height.

Age 6   Yao is already taller than one of his elementary school teachers.

Age 8   Yao is introduced to the sport of basketball. It is an inauspicious debut as he is beaten in foul shooting by a classmate and suffers embarassment.

Age 9   Now stands six feet tall.

Age 12   Because of his height and athleticism, Yao is sent to the Shanghai Juvenile Sports School, a provincial sports academy. He trains several hours a day at the academy, where he lives in a studio dorm room with a king-size bed and private bath. He gets around on an undersized bicycle. Yao doesn't warm to basketball right away but, over time, he begins to enjoy himself in spite of the heavy training regimen.

Age 13   At roughly 6-foot-6, Yao is described as "a crane towering among a flock of chickens."

Age 14   Yao wins a spot on the roster of the Shanghai Oriental Sharks, a team competing in the Chinese Basketball Association's junior league.

Age 15 Is first scouted by the Houston Rockets, his eventual first employer in the NBA.

Age 16 Attends a Nike basketball camp in Paris, France. Begins his professional career in the Chinese Basketball Association with the Shanghai Sharks.

Age 17 Yao is now 7-foot-3. He is named most valuable player at the 14th Asian Basketball Championship for Junior Men in India. Attends Nike's All-America basketball camp in Indianapolis featuring 200 of America's best high school players. Also competes against other AAU junior elite teams across the country while starring for High Five America, a Nike-sponsored AAU squad based in San Diego.

Age 18 Is named to the Chinese national team.

Age 19 Member of China's men's basketball team at the 2000 Olympics in Sydney, Australia. Averages 10.5 points, 6.0 rebounds and 2.2 blocked shots per game during the Olympics.

Age 21 Leads the Shanghai Sharks to their first Chinese Basketball Association title on April 19, 2002, winning a best-of-five final series with the six-time defending champion Bayi Rockets. On June 26, Yao is selected first overall in the 2002 NBA Draft by the Houston Rockets and signs a four-year $18.03 million contract.

NBA Highlights (through game 70 of 82-game 2002-2003 season):

Through March 25, 2003, Yao Ming has averaged 13.8 points (22.5 points per 48 minutes), 8.4 rebounds, 1.6 assists, 1.8 blocks and 29.5 minutes per game. His .517 shooting percentage ranks him sixth in the league and he is 15th in the league in blocks. From November 9 to 21, Yao had the highest field goal percentage in NBA history over a six-game stretch, making 31 of his 35 shot attempts (.886). Yao made his NBA regular-season debut in the Houston Rockets' opener against the Indiana Pacers on October 30, 2002. He finished with no points and two rebounds in 11 minutes of play. Yao broke out with an NBA rookie season-high 30 points and an NBA rookie season-high 16 rebounds on November 21 against Dallas. This was also his first career double-double. His first career start came the next night against the Washington Wizards. Yao's second double-double came on December 3 against San Antonio with 27 points and a career-high 18 rebounds. On December 18 against the Pacers, he had a career-high six blocks along with his 29 points and 10 rebounds. Yao has notched 16 double-doubles to-date. Yao was the first rookie to be named a starter for the All-Star Game since Grant Hill in 1995. Yao received 1,286,324 votes to Shaquille O'Neal's 1,049,081 in the voting for Western Conference centers. Was the only rookie named to *The Sporting News'* 2003 list of the NBA's top 25 players (based on a poll of the league's general managers).

Season	Games Played	Field Goal Percentage	Rebounds Per Game	Blocks Per Game	Assists Per Game	Points Per Game
2002-03	70	.517	8.4	1.8	1.6	13.8

Chinese Basketball Association (CBA) Highlights:

Over his five seasons with the Shanghai Sharks, Yao averaged 23.4 points (on .651 shooting) and 15.4 rebounds in 122 games. During the 2000-2001 CBA season, Yao averaged 27.1 points (on .678 shooting), 19.4 rebounds and 5.5 blocked shots. He also won the CBA's MVP award, finishing third in the league in scoring. In his final season in the CBA (2001-2002), Yao led the league in blocked shots (4.8 blocks per game), and ranked second in scoring (32.4-point average on .721 shooting) and rebounding (19 rebounds per game). He also won the league's sportsmanship award. In helping the Sharks earn their first CBA title, he was truly dominant, averaging 41.3 points, 21 rebounds and 4.3 blocks over the four-game final series against the defending champion Bayi Rockets. In the title-clinching victory, Yao turned in a stunning performance, draining every one of the 21 shots he took that night for a total of 44 points, along with 21 rebounds and seven blocks. On January 5, 2003, Yao became the first Chinese athlete to have his number retired when the Shanghai Sharks retired his number 15 jersey.

Season	Games Played	Field Goal Percentage	Rebounds Per Game	Blocks Per Game	Assists Per Game	Points Per Game
1997-98	21	.615	8.3		0.6	10.0
1998-99	12	.585	12.9	2.5	0.6	20.9
1999-00	33	.585	14.6	5.3	1.7	21.2
2000-01	22	.678	19.4	5.5	2.2	27.1
2001-02	34	.721	19.0	4.3	3.0	32.4

International Competition Highlights:

Yao was a member of China's men's basketball team at the 2000
Olympics in Sydney, Australia. He averaged 10.5 points (on .639
shooting), 6.0 rebounds and 2.2 blocked shots per game during
the Olympics. In July 2001 at the Asian Basketball Championship
for Men held in Shanghai, Yao led the Chinese team to the title,
averaging 13.4 points (on .724 shooting), 10.1 rebounds and 2.8
blocked shots in 20 minutes per game. He was named the
tournament's MVP and Top Rebounder. The next month, at the
2001 World University Games in Beijing, Yao led China to a silver
medal, racking up 15.6 points, 12.4 rebounds and 3.6 blocks per
game. During the semifinals, Yao and his teammates gained an
historic victory in defeating a U.S. team comprised of top college
players, 83-82. The loss ended the Americans' 46-game winning
streak at the World University Games. In achieving the win, the
Chinese team fought its way back from an 11-point deficit late in
the game and Yao made a critical block as time expired. At the
2002 FIBA World Basketball Championship for Men held in
Indianapolis, Yao was named to the All-Tournament Team,
averaging 21.0 points (on .753 shooting), 9.3 rebounds and a
tournament-leading 2.3 blocks for the Chinese team.

Olympics (Sydney)	Games Played	Field Goal Percentage	Rebounds Per Game	Blocks Per Game	Assists Per Game	Points Per Game
2000	6	.639	6.0	2.2	1.7	10.5

THE SKINNY:

Height: **7 feet, 5 inches**

Weight: **296 pounds**

Shoe size: **18**

Shirt size: **XXXX Large (the sleeves are still seven inches too short)**

Wingspan: **90 inches**

Standing upward reach, flat-footed: **9 feet, 7 inches (5 inches below an NBA rim)**

Body fat percentage: **7%**

Neck: **16 inches**

Chest: **42 inches**

Waist: **36 inches**

Thigh: **26 inches**

Houston Rockets jersey number: **11**

Nickname (NBA): **Dynasty**

Nicknames (CBA): **Little Giant; The Golden Bridge; The Moving Great Wall (along with Wang ZhiZhi and Mengke Bateer)**

Websites:

http://www.yaoming.net

http://www.yaomingfanclub.org

http://www.yaomingmania.com

http://www.chinayao.com

THE PHAT:

Yao's favorite activities: sleep, reading and computer games (including Starcraft, Counter-Strike, Medal of Honor and Red Alert).

Yao's favorite American foods are steak, chicken wings and pizza and his favorite Chinese foods are his mother's chicken soup and pork chops.

Favorite drinks: Gatorade and Starbucks iced latte and Frappuccino.

Favorite pop stars: Jay Zhou Jielun and David Yao.

Sleeps in a nine-foot bed the Rockets arranged to have custom-built for him.

Wears a red string bracelet on his left wrist given to him by his girlfriend, who plays for the Chinese national women's basketball team.

Sent Christmas cards to every Rockets employee even though he himself doesn't celebrate the holiday.

Houston locals Chance McClain and Kevin Ryan penned a tribute to Yao entitled, "It's a Ming Thing," which is sung to the tune of the soccer-fan anthem "Ole, Ole, Ole" and has received heavy radio airplay in Houston.

His interpreter, Colin Pine, is a graduate of James Madison University in Virginia and was selected from among 360 applicants for the position.

Yao currently lives in a four-bedroom house in a Houston suburb with both his mother and Pine, who helps out with driving duties as well as round-the-clock language assistance.

One source of confusion for Yao during his first week in Houston was being repeatedly met with the all-purpose greeting "What's up?"; the phrase sounds very similar to a common Mandarin profanity.

Yao, who is used to commuting by bicycle, is having a bike custom-made for him by Jeff Nielsen of West U Schwinn in Houston. Nielsen, who has also built custom bikes for former Rockets Hakeem Olajuwon and Charles Barkley, indicated that Yao's bike would be the biggest he has ever made, including Olajuwon's, which featured a 34-inch frame (the biggest bikes sold in shops have 23-inch frames).

Shanghai-based *Life Weekly* magazine has a regular column called "Keeping Tabs on Yao Ming," which chronicles everything from Yao's on-court exploits to his eating preferences.

China Central Television's telecast of Yao's NBA debut game against the Indiana Pacers on October 30, 2002 reached 287 million households across China; by comparison, there are only around 105 million TV households in the U.S.

In the U.S., Yao's first head-to-head contest with Shaquille O'Neal drew the second-highest cable ratings in NBA history.

Yao's salary in China while playing for the Shanghai Sharks: approximately $80,000.

Yao's salary for his rookie year with the Houston Rockets: $3.8 million.

Yao's chat room pseudonym in his late teens: Sabonis (after Arvydas Sabonis, Lithuanian basketball legend and current Portland Trail Blazer center).

{1}
How Ya Like Me Yao?

Hubie Brown, head coach of the Memphis Grizzlies, recently remarked, "Anybody who criticized him his first couple of weeks in the league has egg on their face now. He's gotten nothing but better, and he's going to keep getting better."

Memphis Commercial Appeal, December 13, 2002

About two years ago, international scouting pioneer and current Dallas Mavericks president of basketball operations Donnie Nelson was watching a Chinese national team practice in downtown Dallas. The Chinese squad featured Wang ZhiZhi, who had been selected by the Mavericks in the second round of the 1999 NBA Draft and was the first Chinese player ever to play in the NBA. But Nelson's attention was riveted to the presence of another seven-footer on the Chinese team: "I'm gonna get me that one," said Donnie, pointing at the tallest player on the floor. "Wang might turn out to be OK," Donnie continued, "but the next great player in the NBA, and the world, is that one over there." "Oh, yeah? What's his name?", he was asked.

"Yao Ming. He's 19 years old," was the reply.

Forth Worth Star-Telegram, January 21, 2003

Terry Rhoads, Nike's director of marketing for China, describing his initial exposure to Yao Ming in China in 1997 when Yao was a 7-foot-3 teenager with three-point shooting range and then, later that year, at a Nike summer camp in Paris:

"Our guys in the U.S. didn't believe that there was a Chinese kid that tall. Once we convinced them, they invited us to bring him to a Nike camp in Paris that summer," said Rhoads. "This was the first time he was matching up against players his own age, and he stood out. Del Harris, then the Lakers coach, was at the camp, and he fell in love with Yao. He was telling everybody, 'I gotta get a picture with that kid because one day he's gonna have a real impact in the NBA.'"

ESPN The Magazine, December 25, 2000

Morris "Bucky" Buckwalter, former Portland Blazers general manager and early proponent of scouting international talent, has followed Yao for several years and and has seen him match up against former NBA greats such as Moses Malone and Kareem Abdul-Jabbar. Said Buckwalter, "He is an outstanding young man. He's not just 7-5 but a talented, active athlete, and the guy is mentally tough. He has great ambition to succeed in the NBA, and he is going to."

"Eventually, he will become the best big man ever to play in the NBA," predicted Buckwalter.

Portland Tribune, August 20, 2002

On October 28, 2002, two days before the opening of the 2002-2003 NBA season, Houston Rockets owner Leslie Alexander boldly declared, **"This is the biggest individual sports story in the world. There are 2 billion Asian people, and everybody's watching it . . . In two years he'll be bigger than Michael [Jordan] ever was, worldwide, and bigger than Tiger [Woods]. I think he's going to be the No. 1 icon in the world."**

USA Today, October 28, 2002

To the chagrin of his hopeful fans, and, seemingly, placing some of the bold, early projections of his impact at risk, Yao struggled at the outset of his NBA debut campaign. He went scoreless in the Rockets' opener against the Pacers and then followed that up with point totals of two, eight, zero and three in his next four games, respectively. Yao's detractors and naysayers began making their voices heard in earnest at this point in his rookie season. One *New York Daily News* reporter made the following observation in early November: **"The Rockets gambled on Yao Ming in the draft and so far it's looking like they crapped out."**

A reporter for the *Arizona Republic* compared Yao to LaRue Martin, the number one pick in the 1972 NBA Draft and thought by many to be the biggest flop in NBA draft history: **"[I]nside of three or four years, he'll probably be history. It also brings to mind an interesting question: How do you say LaRue Martin in Chinese?"**

Arizona Republic, November 15, 2002
New York Daily News, November 10, 2002

In his column for ESPN.com, Bill Simmons criticized the Houston Rockets' decision to choose Yao Ming instead of current Chicago Bulls point guard Jay Williams with the first pick in the draft. He wrote, **"Years from now, we will remember 'Yao Ming over Jay Williams' the same way we remember 'Bowie over Jordan,' 'Traylor for Nowitzki,' 'Carroll for McHale and Parish,' 'Aguirre over Thomas' and every other great draft day blunder in NBA history. I'm not just predicting it, I'm guaranteeing it."**

Exactly six months later, Simmons had this to say: **"I'm an idiot. Forget about Yao's emergence as the most polished rookie big man since Brad Daugherty, or that he offers the first worthy challenge to Shaq since Hakeem was still The Dream. If you're a basketball fan, you love Yao Ming."**

ESPN.com, June 27, 2002
ESPN.com, December 27, 2002

11-time All-Star and former Rocket Charles Barkley on November 14, 2002 after Yao's sixth game: **"Yao Ming makes [7-foot-6 NBA journeyman] Shawn Bradley look like Bill Russell. He might be a good player some day, but he is not ready."**

During the same *Inside the NBA* telecast, Barkley, the show's colorful host, put his mouth where his mouth was by further declaring to his national television audience that if Yao Ming were to score as many as 19 points in an NBA game during his rookie season, **"I am going to kiss [co-host] Kenny's ass."** When news of the wager was incorrectly communicated to Yao causing him to mistakenly believe himself to be the prospective recipient of the kiss, Yao, with characteristic good humor, fired back, **"Better stop at 18 in that case."**

To many, Barkley's boast seemed well-founded given that Yao had averaged just over three points per game to that point.

It only took three days for Yao to make Barkley eat his words. In his first game against the LA Lakers, he shot 9-for-9 from the field, scoring 20 points in just 23 minutes of play. The future Hall of Famer Barkley proved to be true to his word. November 20, on CNN's *TalkBack Live* program, Barkley vowed, "I am going to pay up [Thursday] night. If you make a bet, you pay up. I just told Kenny to take a shower before the show. I made the bet and I'm going to stick by my word. Ugh." Co-host Kenny Smith deadpanned in reply, "Sometimes even when you win, you lose."

Even Michael Jordan got in on the fun, observing, "Any time you can make Charles Barkley kiss an ass, that's a good thing. I just couldn't tell which one was the ass. Was it a four-legged ass or a two-legged ass?"

When the appointed time came for Barkley to make good on his promise, on TNT's *Stand Up!* pregame show prior to the Rockets-Mavericks contest, it was Smith who balked as he arranged instead for Barkley to kiss the posterior of Shorty, a male donkey Smith had rented for $500 from a ranch near Atlanta. After the game, a humbled Barkley offered the following clarification: "Kenny said that I said Yao Ming couldn't play, and that's inaccurate. You don't want the Chinese mad at you. They can fight. I thought he would be good. I just didn't think it would be this soon."

Inside the NBA on TNT, November 14, 2002
Sacramento Bee, December 10, 2002
Houston Chronicle, November 23, 2002

The day before an exhibition game between the Chinese and U.S. national teams in August 2002, Ben Wallace, the reigning NBA Defensive Player of the Year, crowed,

"We're going to beat him up. We're going to beat him up pretty bad. Welcome to the league, welcome to our country. This is our playground. This is how we play."

The next day, Wallace was singing a different song:

"He's got a nice touch and a couple of post moves, a couple of good moves around the basket," said Wallace. "As long as he continues to play [like] he was playing, he's going to continue to grow as a player. To my surprise, he was a whole lot better than I thought he was."

Detroit Free Press, August 22, 2002
USA Basketball.com, August 22, 2002

Speaking eloquently to one aspect of the pressure on Yao to not disappoint the many Asian and Asian American fans for whom Yao has become an "overthrower" of stereotypes and a living symbol of their cultural pride, one Asian American fan offered the following insight: **"There was so much hype around him, if he blows it, it's my small internal battle magnified a thousand times."**

A recent issue of China's *Life Week* magazine referred to Yao as "a symbol of Chinese identity in an era of globalization."

Associated Press, February 8, 2003
National Public Radio, February 7, 2003

As Yao accelerated his level of play in the second half of November and throughout December, routinely posting double-doubles, the tide of public opinion began to turn. NBA Hall of Famer and Bay Area basketball legend Rick Barry, at the beginning of December 2002: **"I hate to say I told you so, but I really did. For two years, I have said that Yao Ming can flat out play. At his size, he is the best player I have ever seen and I believe that he will leave a lasting mark on the NBA. So far, he has exhibited an exceptional shooting touch, instinctive passing ability and a mental approach to the game that will guarantee his success. The other skills necessary to be a major force at the center position will come with time. Write this down: Yao Ming will be the first of many big men from China to make an impact in the NBA."**

San Francisco Examiner, December 4, 2002

NBA Hall of Famer and ESPN and ABC lead NBA commentator Bill Walton, on Yao: "When I watch Yao Ming play, I'm reminded of Magic Johnson. He makes plays like Garry Kasparov, like Bobby Fischer [both chess champions]. You sit there and say, 'No way he thought of that. That had to be luck.' [Larry] Bird was that way, too — always so far ahead of everyone else mentally."

Walton added, "As Yao Ming develops into more of an NBA player, the anticipation I have for what is to come . . . I'm so excited about the whole thing. There is no limit to what he can accomplish. Yao Ming has the potential, the capability, of changing the future of basketball."

Walton on Yao, once more: "Is there any thing Yao Ming can't do? We all have so much to learn from him. Why does everybody think it's the other way around?"

Houston Chronicle, December 18, 2002
ESPN.com, December 24, 2002

Prior to a game against Houston, former Rocket and current Atlanta Hawks guard Emanual Davis remarked, "You want to know about Yao Ming? Let me tell you what the NBA players think about Yao Ming. All you need to know is that every player in the league wants to see him play. They're all talking about Yao Ming, and everybody wants to see him play. How many players can you say that about? He's looking like a young Dream [Hakeem Olajuwon]. He has great feet, good hands and he has a good sense of how the game should be played."

Houston Chronicle, December 21, 2002

The Miami Heat's standout rookie forward Caron Butler was asked about a photo of Butler completely dwarfed by the much-larger Yao Ming. The photo captures the 6-foot-7-inch Butler jumping up into Yao's armpit. Said Butler, "He's huge. It's like playing against a tree. Everywhere you look, he's got you within reach. He's so long, so athletic and he's got a good basketball IQ, so it's like he can reach you from everywhere."

Miami Herald, February 21, 2003

After a January 8 game between the Rockets and the Orlando Magic in which Yao had 23 points and 11 rebounds, current NBA scoring leader Tracy McGrady said, "He's going to be a great player in this league once he gets some games under his belt. And once he gets comfortable with the game he's going to be unbelievable. He just takes so much out of you because he's so big and hard to double team because he can just look over the defense and pass out with ease. He's a handful, man."

Florida Today, January 9, 2003

Yao has made a habit of executing baseline spin moves that men his size are not supposed to pull off. In the second quarter of that January 8 matchup with the Magic, Yao left Orlando center Pat Burke flat-footed as he first dribbled, then spun away from Burke's trap in the corner and drove to the basket in a fluid, quicksilver sequence more befitting a young Michael Jordan than a 7-foot-5, 296-pound rookie center. Said Burke after the game, **"Two steps, and he is at the basket. I tell you what, I won't trap him in the corner again. I did not think he could put it on the floor like that. He dribbled, what, one time? I guess he proved me wrong."**

Sporting News, January 17, 2003

7-foot-1 future Hall of Fame center David Robinson, who was named in 1996 to the list of the 50 greatest NBA players of all time, said, **"There aren't too many guys who have made me feel short, but, wow, he's big. He made me feel short and small."**

Los Angeles Times, November 17, 2002

His Airness Michael Jordan, widely considered to be the greatest basketball player of all time, had this to say after his Washington Wizards played their first game against Yao Ming: **"He's for real. Look at that 30 and 16 [the 30 points and 16 rebounds he tallied against Dallas]. He's getting better and better."**

Yao on Jordan, after an overtime loss to Jordan's Washington Wizards, in which Jordan lit the Rockets up for 35 points: **"Right now I hope that he hurries up and retires — we would then be able to play more relaxed."**

NBA.com, January 22, 2003
Associated Press, February 27, 2003

Yao's uncommon agility for his height prompted 2001 NBA MVP Allen Iverson to gush, **"He's special. He's a gift from God."**

Time Magazine, February 5, 2003

{2}
You Say Tomato
I Say Fan Qie

While chowing down on a sirloin and rib combo at a
Shanghai outpost of a famous U.S. restaurant chain, Yao
shared the following thoughts about eating in America:
"I like big steaks. And I like going to
Starbucks. The food in Chinese restaurants
there is different than here. It was strange
seeing a fortune cookie for the first time.
We don't have them here. Must be an
American invention."

ESPN The Magazine, December 25, 2000

In a pre-game media session prior to a contest with the Orlando Magic, Yao was asked – as he often is – about his adjustment to life in America. **"One thing I've found in every place I've been to in America,"** he offered, **"there's some Chinese people."**

Orlando Sentinel, January 9, 2003

In explaining how he planned to communicate with his NBA opponents, given his as yet limited English language capabilities, Yao replied, **"I'll use Chinese to trash talk."**

USA Today, October 28, 2002

Yao was asked what he missed most about China.
"Familiarity," he said. "I miss a kind of atmosphere, a kind of familiar atmosphere when I'm not in the gym. Nothing [here] is familiar besides the gym."

Houston Chronicle, December 24, 2002

Asked about making adjustments to life in America in terms of both diet and language, Yao replied, "I think it's probably more difficult for me to adjust to the diet than the language." He went on, "I think I have to say 'sorry' to my stomach and let it get used to it and practice a little, let my stomach practice a little with American food."

ESPN.com, September 3, 2002

Asked what he knew about the American Thanksgiving tradition, Yao replied, "I have heard of the turkey that is at the center of this meal. I have tasted some of it before, maybe sliced up or in pieces. But I have never seen a whole turkey served for a meal. And I have definitely never eaten a whole turkey . . . You tell me about all of these things that we will have, so maybe I will decide not to eat all day until we sit down for the dinner."

Houston Chronicle, November 28, 2002

Regarding his eating habits here in the U.S., Yao commented, "I try to eat a lot of Chinese food. Up until yesterday, I've been able to eat my mother's cooking almost every day. Obviously when I'm on the road, I can't eat my mother's cooking, because my interpreter can't cook."

SI.com, November 15, 2002

Perceptive about his role as a goodwill ambassador to the United States for his home country of China, Yao commented, "I hope I am a good textbook. It seems to me I am here to do more than play basketball. You have to understand that in China there is a lot of emphasis on collective honor and the honor of the entire country. I'd like Americans to see how Chinese people really work hard in difficult situations. I hope that, through my work in the NBA, they can see that."

USA Today, October 28, 2002

A reporter for *China Sports Weekly*, China's biggest sports magazine, on how Yao has represented his homeland:

"Yao has given a new Chinese image. People thought of Chinese people as short and skinny, not fierce, unable to play competitive sports. Yao has shown that is wrong. But he's also stayed kind and friendly and warm. I think a lot of people know that about him now."

Sports Illustrated, January 27, 2003

Underwhelmed by the Miami Heat's promotion featuring commemorative fortune cookies for fans attending the Heat's first matchup with the Yao-led Rockets, Yao commented, **"First of all, there's no such thing as a fortune cookie in China."** Then, laughing at the size of the freebie, the 7-foot-5 center added, **"I think fortune cookies are too small. I think you have to go a little bigger,"** suggesting instead a barbecued pork delicacy.

Forth Worth Star-Telegram, December 22, 2002

Asked whether he had received any advice on living in America from the first two Chinese basketball players to play in the NBA, Wang ZhiZhi and Mengke Bateer, Yao replied, **"Mengke told me I have to learn to drive a car (laughs). I don't have a driver's license yet. I only had a bicycle in Shanghai."**

FIBA.com, August 8, 2002

While still in China, Yao was asked for his thoughts on playing in the U.S. in the near future. He remarked, "If I do play in the States, the Chinese friends to me are very important. Anyone staying out of his country feels a strong attachment to his own country and people."

San Francisco Examiner, March 5, 2002

Thirty minutes before Yao Ming even appeared at his designated table at the 2003 All-Star Game media interview session, there were already 50 reporters patiently waiting for the NBA's newest star. During the session, Yao was asked about the significance of his outfit of the Chinese national team's black pants and black jersey. He replied, **"It's to show that I really miss my audience and friends in China."**

Philadelphia Inquirer, February 9, 2003

Yao still has much of the English language to master; however, he demonstrated that he is picking up the hoops jargon just fine during one particular sequence of a January matchup with the Orlando Magic that had tongues wagging. After taking a hard foul on the arms by Shawn Kemp, Yao turned, arm muscles flexed, and shouted, **"And one!!,"** as his hook shot banked off the glass and fell through the net.

Atlanta Journal-Constitution, January 9, 2003

{3}
Everything's Bigger in Texas

On fan support at games in Houston, Yao said, "What has really touched me is that they haven't just looked at me as a basketball player. They've treated me like a Texan and really taken me into their hearts."

USA Today, October 28, 2002

Yao was asked how important it was to be coming to play in Houston, knowing that it has such a substantial Asian community. He replied, **"The fact that there are so many Chinese people in Houston will make me feel more at home. It will help out a lot."**

NBA.com, October 20, 2002

Asked what he knew about the city of Houston prior to being drafted by the Rockets, Yao responded, "I know they have won two NBA championships. I know Houston is a very large city with a large Asian population. And I also know Houston is a very young team, similar to the team that I'm on currently in China. And that's the type of team with great potential."

ESPN.com, September 3, 2002

Asked about the kind of welcome he has received in Texas, Yao said, **"The city has given me a very warm feeling. Whenever anybody greets me, they treat me like I'm a Texan, a new Texan."** Yao, who is from the fourth largest city in the world, went on to recall his prior experience of Texas, adding, **"I've been in Dallas before . . . and my impression was, 'It's really hot in the summer, the steak is really good, the area is very large and the cities aren't that crowded.'"**

Thinking back on the first NBA game he ever saw on television – a Knicks-Rockets matchup in the '94 Finals: **"I was rooting for Houston,"** Yao said. **"Everybody on the team I was on in Shanghai was rooting for the Knicks so I was rooting for the Rockets."**

New York Post, December 27, 2002

Rockets trainer Keith Jones recalled how the team was first exposed to Yao's dry sense of humor in recounting a trip to China by team doctor Walter Lowe to examine Yao's foot prior to the 2002 NBA Draft:

"Yao was asking about Houston, and Dr. Lowe was saying what a great town it was, how it has more restaurants than any American city except New York. He told Yao, 'We've got some great Chinese restaurants, great Chinese food.' Yao paused and then retorted playfully, 'How would you know? You're not Chinese.'"

Associated Press, February 5, 2003

Banter between Yao and his everpresent translator/sidekick Colin Pine as they drove from basketball practice to a television commercial photo shoot, with Pine at the wheel:

"Traffic in Houston sucks," said Pine.

"Traffic in Houston is normal," said the more cosmopolitan Yao, whose hometown has almost 15 million residents.

On the gastronomic appeals of the Lone Star State: **"I like steak. That's why I came to Texas."**

USA Today, October 28, 2002

{ 4 }
Rookie Year Confidential

While in the U.S. for a two-day basketball tournament, an 18-year-old Yao Ming made his feelings known about the prospect of one day testing his talents in the NBA. Said Yao, **"I don't know if I'll be able to go or not but I want to. I don't care if I'm the first Chinese player in the NBA or the second or the third. I just want to try it."**

AsianBasketball.com, September 17, 1999

Yao's mother Fang Feng Di, commenting on how she and Yao's father are uniquely positioned to provide helpful counsel to Yao through difficult times due to their having played center during their respective basketball careers:

"We understand that training can be really tiring because we've been through that. When the going gets tough, we exchange ideas with him, give him some suggestions and some encouragement since we were centers too."

Shanghai Star, September 15, 2000

When asked in December 2000 what most surprised him about the experience of playing basketball in America, primarily at summer camps, Yao pointed to the emotion and passion expressed via the dunk and how, in China, players rarely dunked the ball, preferring instead to lay it in. Yao related the account of how, frustrated with this reserved style of play from him, one of his American coaches told him, "If you get the ball in close and don't dunk it, all of your teammates are going to have to run laps." "But I couldn't help it," said Yao, "I was very accustomed to laying the ball in the basket. All of my teammates were running laps, begging me to dunk. Finally, after about a week and many laps, I began to dunk it every time."

ESPN The Magazine, December 25, 2000

Upon referring to an Asian junior championship game in which he had an astonishing 17 blocks as his most memorable on-court experience, Yao was next asked whether he would rather have 30 blocks or 30 points in a game. He replied, **"I'd take the 30 blocks. If you have 30 blocks it will destroy your opponents' morale. It will take away their heart."**

ESPN The Magazine, December 25, 2000a

In a statement made by Yao after a pre-draft workout in Chicago attended by representatives from 26 NBA teams and over 150 members of the media, Yao said, "It's been a dream of mine to play in the NBA ever since the first time I saw a game on TV many years ago. To almost touch that dream today fills me with a sense of joy that words simply cannot describe."

Sydney Morning Herald, May 3, 2002

Asked who he looked forward to competing against in the NBA, Yao said, **"Shaq. Olajuwon. Sabonis. Tim Duncan. David Robinson. A lot."**

ESPN.com, September 3, 2002

Asked how he expected to make the adjustment from the Chinese game, which emphasizes the primacy of the team over the individual far more than in the NBA, Yao replied, "I think I'll stick to what I'm used to, my principle, and that is team No. 1 and individual No. 2. I remember going to an NBA training facility, and I remember seeing a very large letter on the wall, saying 'no one's bigger than the team.'"

ESPN.com, September 3, 2002

Following a preseason contest against the San Antonio Spurs, Yao had the following to say about his first experience playing in the NBA: **"When you watch it on TV it seems really easy. But when you are actually out there playing, it is extremely difficult."**

Associated Press, October 25, 2002

After his first NBA regular season game against the Indiana Pacers on October 30, 2002, in which he failed to score a point in 11 minutes of playing time, Yao remarked, "I learned I still have a lot to learn and I am just a rookie. I realize this is only the beginning. There are some things I regret. It was disappointing. But there has to be a start for everything and this is a start for me."

Agence France-Presse, November 1, 2002

Yao added the following comments after his debut against the Pacers, expressing disappointment while maintaining a confident outlook on his career in the NBA: **"In all aspects, it felt like a war,"** said Yao of his initiation into the NBA. He added, **"I was a little bit sorry for my performance, but that's the reality I have to face. I will have my value recognized in several years."**

People's Daily, October 31, 2002

Commenting on playing against 7-foot-6 Shawn Bradley after scoring 30 points in a losing effort against the Dallas Mavericks, Yao said, **"I don't get many chances to play against a player as tall as me, so I was very excited."** He added, **"Now I know I'm not the skinniest player in the NBA."**

Associated Press, November 21, 2002

Asked for his reaction to the publicity surrounding Charles Barkley's on-air promise to kiss his co-host's posterior if Yao managed to score 19 points in a game this season, Yao graciously sidestepped the controversy while proving to be a good sport, saying, **"It's a little strange to me that people pay attention to things outside the game, rather than the competition itself, but that's not to say it's not fun. I knew that Charles and other people in the NBA like to joke around. I didn't think I would be the focus of the jokes so quickly."**

Houston Chronicle, November 22, 2002

On playing against the San Antonio Spurs with their two seven-footers Tim Duncan and David Robinson, Yao said,

"I knew that I was going against two great centers. They play very strong inside. I knew I had to fight a little harder for rebounds. It was my one arm going up against two of theirs."

Houston Chronicle, December 4, 2002

In his typically self-deprecating manner, Yao attempted to ratchet down some of the skyrocketing expectations following on the heels of some of his early-season successes, saying, "I read some Chinese reports on the website. They always said like, 'Yao Ming is accustomed with NBA' after I played one or two good games. Is NBA that easy? NBA is not just one or two games."

Xinhua News Agency, December 7, 2002

On the benefit of having his mother living with him during his rookie year in the NBA, Yao said, **"No matter what challenges and hardships are outside, it's really nice to have a warm home to come back to."**

ESPN.com, December 18, 2002

On adjusting to the grueling, 82-game NBA regular season from a routine he had known in China where the standard regular season runs only 34 games, Yao said, **"The NBA season is definitely different than anywhere else. From the length of the season to the physicality and the rules of the game, all of it's been a test for me. It's been a lot harder than I ever expected. Not only on the basketball court, but everything else, too. Especially the travelling and having to go from city to city."**

Florida Today, January 8, 2003

Alluding to the notable differences in height, athleticism and jumping ability, on average, between the players in the Chinese Basketball Association and the NBA, Yao, commenting on the adjustments he had had to make in order to score in the NBA, said, **"A lot of times I have to use the hook shot. It depends on the defender. A lot of times that's the only way I can get my shot off. If there's an opportunity, I'll use it, but it's not a shot I used much when I was in China. I didn't need to use it there."**

Houston Chronicle, January 25, 2003

Toward the midpoint of his first season in the NBA, a point at which many rookies begin to experience fatigue, Yao was asked, after a 14-point, eight-rebound performance against the Bulls in which he seemed sluggish, whether he had hit the "rookie wall." Yao answered, **"I'm only a rookie. I don't know what the rookie wall is. You'll be able to tell before I will."**

Chicago Sun-Times, January 27, 2003

Responding to more questions about whether he had hit the "rookie wall," Yao conceded, "I've never been through something like this before. I don't know if this is what you'd call tired or not. It's like if you've never been drunk before and you get drunk for the first time, you don't know that you're drunk. But I'm definitely pretty exhausted in some games."

Los Angeles Times, February 2, 2003

Asked how he suddenly began to play like an All-Star after his first few forgettable performances at the beginning of the season, Yao said, with characteristic humility,

"I don't know what happened. It's a testament to my coaches and teammates. They've helped me very much."

Time Magazine, February 5, 2003

Commenting on the experience of being the number one object of media interest during the NBA All-Star Weekend – even with Michael Jordan playing in his final All-Star game – Yao, who has endured relentless worldwide media attention every day of his rookie season, remarked, **"The last three days, it has been a carousel. It has been turning round and round all the time."**

And then when asked to name his favorite moment from his All-Star experience, he replied, simply, **"When I was in my room."**

Star-Ledger, February 10, 2003

On October 24, 2002, former president George Bush hosted a dinner in Crawford, Texas in honor of Chinese President Jiang Zemin. Many prominent political figures and other persons-of-note were in attendance. As the various dignitaries – including some heads of state – were introduced, the applause was polite but restrained. When Yao Ming was introduced, however, the response of Bush's dinner guests changed dramatically to boisterous and sustained cheering. When the ovation finally died down – reportedly some minutes later – Bush, proud to have Yao in Texas, turned to Jiang and marveled, **"You're the second most recognizable Chinese face in America now."**

Washington Post, February 28, 2003

{5}
I'm a
Rocket Man

Glen Rice, teammate to Shaquille O'Neal for two seasons and current teammate of Yao Ming, on Yao's mental toughness: **"You cannot break this guy's spirit. Shaq will do what he always does. But this guy [Yao] always gets back up. And he learns from it. I saw this in the very beginning. Mentally, he just gets stronger and stronger. You cannot break him."**

Houston Chronicle, January 16, 2003

Despite Yao's superstar status with the media and among the fans, his teammates have helped to keep him grounded by refusing to give him a free pass on standard rookie duties in the NBA, including delivering veteran players' game shoes when on the road, carrying teammates' bags and arriving early to practice. Said teammate and veteran NBA forward Glen Rice, "We're going to work him hard in practice, and we're going to work him hard carrying bags. He can be 8-foot-9, and we're still going to give him the rookie treatment. We can hang a lot of bags on him." Yao replied, smiling, **"A rookie has to do what a rookie has to do."**

USA Today, October 28, 2002

Yao, on getting his teammates involved in the offense:

"When I'm seeing them score points, it feels like I'm scoring points myself."

NBA.com, December 10, 2002

Shortly after hearing teammate Moochie Norris walk past him outside the locker room singing an improvised song with his name in it, Yao remarked quietly, **"It makes me feel they really welcome me and helped me become a part of this team."**

Houston Chronicle, December 8, 2002

Asked about whether he has had any difficulties communicating with teammates on the court, Yao said, **"I can understand most of them on the court. I talk a lot with them during the games. But sometimes the Chinese just jumped out,"** giggled Yao.

Xinhua News Agency, December 7, 2002

After the Rockets' December 18 game against the Pacers –
a game in which Yao had 29 points, 10 boards and six
blocks — team captain and scoring leader Steve Francis,
commenting on Yao's importance to the team, said, **"We
had to keep the ball inside. It was obvious
he was dominating the game."** Francis added,
**"Cuttino [Mobley] missed four in a row,
Glen [Rice] missed three in a row. I missed
two in a row. We said we're going to live
and die with what [Yao] does for us."**

Houston Chronicle, December 19, 2002

Houston Rockets coach Rudy Tomjanovich, after Yao's December 18 performance against the Pacers: **"Yao is so inspiring,"** said Tomjanovich. **"It just gives me goose bumps sometimes after he makes a play, to hear that buzz in the crowd, people saying, 'Could you believe that?' It was reminiscent of when Dream [Hakeem Olajuwon] was here."**

Chicago Sun-Times, December 22, 2002

Rockets general manager Carroll Dawson, on how much the team coveted Yao: "We've followed him since he was 14 . . . There was no question in our minds. We never had a doubt. From the moment we got the first pick in the lottery, I told everybody who called and wanted to trade for the pick: 'No, we're keeping it. We're taking Yao Ming.' There was no controversy about it, ever."

Globe and Mail, September 3, 2002

Commenting on Yao's team-first attitude, Rockets point guard Steve Francis observed, "He's not like an American player. All these cameras following him around, he could care less about them." Added Francis, "He's the first one in the gym, last one out. Always."

ESPN The Magazine, December 3, 2002

Francis, on how he feels about his relationship with Yao:

"I know he's younger than me, but I think he's my big brother already."

"He's just like me, except 7-foot-5 and Chinese," said Francis.

Philadelphia Daily News, November 8, 2002
Houston Chronicle, December 24, 2002

Francis, who is an NBA superstar in his own right, has demonstrated wisdom and maturity in not begrudging Yao his involuntary celebrity status. Instead of keeping the newcomer at arm's length, Francis has embraced Yao with gusto, nicknaming him "Dynasty" and planning a new line of gear under his clothing label to honor his new friend and teammate. On the court, Francis even uses a bit of self-taught Mandarin in order to help Yao overcome his [traditionally Chinese] aversion to dunking by yelling **"Zhudong yedian!"**, which means, roughly, "Be more aggressive!"

Newsday, February 9, 2003

Rockets shooting guard Cuttino Mobley, on how he feels about Yao and why he is comfortable with Yao getting the lion's share of the spotlight since his arrival: **"I'll tell you why I'm cool with it,"** explained Mobley. **"Because you can't deny that what we needed was a big man. And that man right there [Mobley points at Yao] is the real deal. The other part of it is, Yao is one great dude. Not cocky. Modest. Loving. Always hugging you. Always wanting to learn."**

Sports Illustrated, January 27, 2003

Rockets reserve point guard Moochie Norris, on the big man's eyebrow-raising passing ability: **"[W]hen he throws you a pass, a lot of times he has to shout out your name so you know it's coming."**

Sporting News, January 17, 2003

Yao interpreter Colin Pine, on Yao's relations and interactions with his teammates: "He's a great person, has a great attitude, and he's funny. He takes things in stride, and he likes to joke around with his teammates a lot. The one story I've been telling people: We were at shoot-around at the Compaq Center in Houston, and the equipment manager found a baby rat in a shoe. Yao looks over and yells over at [diminutive point guard who is nicknamed "Mouse"] Moochie Norris, and yells in English, 'Hey Moochie, your brother is over here.'"

SportsLine.com, November 27, 2002

Rockets general manager Carroll Dawson, on Yao's attitude:

"He's an incredibly endearing person. He's got this humble demeanor that is refreshing in our sport, and he has the patience of Job." Dawson continued, "I remember the first day he came to practice. He missed all of training camp and most of our preseason because of obligations to his national team. There had been a tremendous amount of hype about him already, so I was curious to see how it went. In the first five minutes, he set three picks, made two terrific passes, and, when he scored, he ran back down the court with his head down. That's all it took. He had won his teammates over."

Boston Globe, January 13, 2003

Though former Rocket and NBA great Charles Barkley is not a current teammate of Yao's, this gem of a quote, though unrelated to Yao, warrants "emeritus" inclusion in this book:

"Tiger and I were in Vegas playing golf not so long ago, and he asked if I'd heard about the new super Kmart store being built there," Barkley recalled. "And I said, 'No, where are they gonna build it?' And Tiger said, 'In the space between your ball and mine.' My God, he even beats me talking trash."

–Charles Barkley, who finished his stellar NBA career with four seasons as a Rocket, on the humbling experience of playing golf with Tiger Woods

USA Today, April 24, 2001

Chinese national team center Yao Ming (13) enters the second half with teammates Li Nan (L), Hu Weidong (8), Guo Shiqiang (4) and Liu Yudong (11) as they played against Team USA in an exhibition game on August 22, 2002 in Oakland, California. The USA defeated China 84-54.

© Reuters NewMedia Inc./CORBIS
REUTERS/Adrees Latif

China's Yao Ming slam-dunks two points against Argentina during round two of the FIBA World Basketball Championship, September 2, 2002 in Indianapolis, Indiana. Argentina defeated China 95-71.

© Reuters NewMedia Inc./CORBIS
REUTERS/Adrees Latif

China's Yao Ming towering over fellow Chinese athletes at a welcoming ceremony on September 27, 2002 at the 14th Asian Games Athletes Village in Pusan, Korea. The teams from 44 countries including Afghanistan and East Timor would take part in the 17-day-long games, participating in 38 sports.

© Reuters NewMedia Inc./CORBIS
REUTERS/Jason Reed

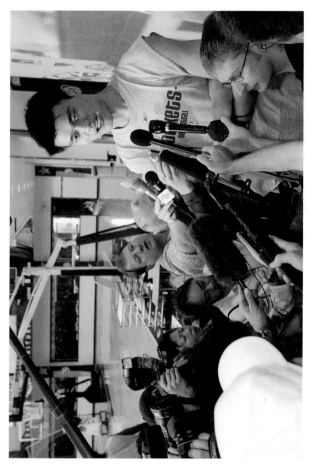

Chinese center Yao Ming, with interpreter Colin Pine at his side, talking to the media during a courtside interview at the Rockets practice facility in Houston on October 21, 2002. Yao, who played for the Shanghai Sharks of the Chinese Basketball Association and the Chinese national team, was the first pick in the 2002 NBA Draft and the first-ever international first round pick in NBA history.

© Reuters NewMedia Inc./CORBIS
REUTERS/Richard Carson

Houston Rockets center Yao Ming (C) learns plays from Rockets assistant coach Jim Boylen (L) and his interpreter Colin Pine (R) at a team practice at the Westside Tennis Club in Houston, Texas on October 21, 2002, the day after Yao's "rock star-like" arrival in his new hometown.

© AFP/CORBIS
AFP PHOTO/James Nielsen

Bare-chested Houston Rockets fans cheer on center Yao
Ming during his first home court appearance in the first
half of the Rockets' preseason game against the
Philadelphia 76ers on October 24, 2002 in Houston.

© Reuters NewMedia Inc./CORBIS
REUTERS/Richard Carson

Houston Rockets guard Steve Francis (L) has the ear of fast friend and Rockets center Yao Ming (R) as the two sit on the bench in the fourth quarter of a game against the Indiana Pacers. The game was Yao's regular season NBA debut and took place on October 30, 2002 at Conseco Fieldhouse in Indianapolis.

© Reuters NewMedia Inc./CORBIS
REUTERS/Brent Smith

Yao Ming of the Houston Rockets slam-dunks two of his 21 first-half points against the Dallas Mavericks at the American Airlines Center in Dallas, Texas on November 21, 2002. He finished the game with 30 points and 16 rebounds.

© AFP/CORBIS
AFP PHOTO/Paul Buck

Yao Ming of the Houston Rockets keeps his eye on the ball under the basket during the first quarter of a game against the San Antonio Spurs at the Compaq Center in Houston, Texas on December 3, 2002.

© AFP/CORBIS
AFP PHOTO/James Nielsen

Houston Rockets' center Yao Ming blocks the shot of Boston
Celtics' guard Paul Pierce (L). The Rockets' Cuttino Mobley
(foreground) looks on as Pierce drives to the basket and gets
rejected by Yao in the first half of the January 13, 2003
Rockets-Celtics matchup in Houston.

© Reuters NewMedia Inc./CORBIS
REUTERS/Richard Carson

Yao Ming (R) of the Houston Rockets posting up against the Boston Celtics' Tony Battie (L) during the fourth quarter of the Rockets-Celtics contest at the Compaq Center in Houston on January 13, 2003.

© AFP/CORBIS
AFP PHOTO/James Nielsen

In the eye of a media hurricane surrounding insensitive remarks made and later apologized for by Shaquille O'Neal, Rockets' center Yao Ming shares a warm greeting with the Lakers' big man before their January 17, 2003 matchup in Houston.

© Reuters NewMedia Inc./CORBIS
REUTERS/Richard Carson

Houston Rockets' center Yao Ming blocks Los Angeles Lakers'
center Shaquille O'Neal's opening shot, sending O'Neal to the floor
in the opening volley of the first match-up between the two players
on January 17, 2003 in Houston.

© Reuters NewMedia Inc./CORBIS
REUTERS/Richard Carson

Los Angeles Lakers guard Kobe Bryant (L) guards rookie center Yao Ming of the Houston Rockets during practice on February 8, 2003 for the 52nd NBA All-Star Game in Atlanta, which was held the next day. Bryant and Yao were both named starters for the Western Conference squad.

© Reuters NewMedia Inc./CORBIS
REUTERS/Tami Chappell

Houston Rocket Cuttino Mobley jumps on the back of fellow teammate Yao Ming after beating the Boston Celtics in overtime 101-95, February 24, 2003.

© Reuters/STRINGER/USA
REUTERS/Stuart Cahill

Houston Rockets center Yao Ming guarding the Rockets' basket
during a game against the Washington Wizards in Washington on
February 27, 2003.

© Reuters NewMedia Inc./CORBIS
REUTERS/Hyungwon Kang

{6}
Me and My Shadow

Of 29-year-old Colin Pine, his live-in interpreter, cultural sherpa, chauffeur and friend, Yao said, **"When the sun comes out, so does my shadow."**

Houston Chronicle, December 24, 2002

Pine, a 5-foot-10-inch Baltimore native and James Madison University graduate, was translating Chinese documents for the State Department when he received an email from a friend informing him about an NBA team looking for a native English speaker fluent in Mandarin. Pine had mastered the language during three years in Taipei and decided to apply. Several months later, after a battery of interviews and translation tests, Pine was selected from a pool of nearly 400 applicants to be Yao Ming's personal translator. On October 3, 2002, he reported for work in Houston.

Just over two weeks later, Pine met Yao for the first time as the Rockets' top draft choice landed at George Bush International Airport in Houston on October 20. As the boyish-looking Pine recalled, the ready-to-wisecrack Yao's first words to him were, "I thought you would be older."

Reflecting on his experience, Pine said, "I was told up front if he doesn't need you after a year, the job is done. The way I look at it is I didn't take the job as a means to an end, but as an experience. I'm enjoying it while it lasts. It's been a dream."

Washington Post, February 27, 2003
Chicago Tribune, January 25, 2003

Pine, sharing his anxieties about possible high-pressure moments in his new job, such as late-game team huddle situations where he would be called on to translate for Yao: "I've had a lot of nightmares about that," Pine said. "I sometimes find myself just thinking about at the end of a game when a play is being drawn up and I'm the guy that's trying to explain to Yao."

Associated Press, October 13, 2002

On having one of the coolest jobs in America: "My friends back in Maryland say they're going to quit their jobs, pack their bags and come to Houston," said Pine. "They're going to be Yao Ming's posse, since he doesn't have one yet. One friend has already claimed the job of holding Yao's cell phone. Another one is going to tie his shoes. This has been crazy."

Houston Chronicle, November 1, 2002

Pine, on the "planned obsolescence" aspect of his job whereby the better he does his job, the sooner he puts himself out of a job: **"I'm rooting for him and hoping he can get rid of me."**

In a separate interview, Pine, whose current contract will expire in June, explained, **"He doesn't want someone speaking for him all the time. What that means for my future, I don't know. Yao and I have become good friends, so it's whatever he wants. If he says he wants me back next year, I'll stay. It's been a great ride no matter what."**

Associated Press, November 13, 2002
Washington Post, February 27, 2003

Although Yao has not yet earned a driver's license, he practices driving in his suburban neighborhood with Pine riding shotgun. During these sessions, Pine quipped, **"I sit in the car and fear for my life . . . Just kidding."**

New York Times, December 15, 2002

Pine, providing a feisty perspective on the challenges and pressures Yao has faced in his brief time in America: "He is really a bright guy, and he understands a lot," said Pine. "But he is not fluent by any means. Imagine if you were dropped into China and had three months to learn the language. Do you think you'd be ready to conduct a press conference?"

Pine, who has been for several months a near-constant companion to Yao – at home, on the road, at games, in the car – explaining how surreal he finds his current life to be:

"I have moments when I'm sitting on the bench or during practice and I think, 'Man, I would be watching this on TV or seeing it on *SportsCenter*.' But there I am, right in the middle."

Chicago Tribune, January 25, 2003

Yao was asked whether his English is better than he lets on. He turned to Pine, grinning, and said in Mandarin, **"I still don't understand a lot of things. If I did, you would have been fired a while ago."**

Time Magazine, February 5, 2003

At a press conference in November in which reporters
explained the American tradition of Thanksgiving to Yao,
the Rockets center was asked what he was thankful for.
Yao put his arm around Pine, smiled, and said, "My
interpreter, Colin." Pine blushed.

ESPN The Magazine, December 3, 2002

{7}
Shaq, Who's Yao Daddy?

"Hey Shaq, who's Yao daddy?" and **"Yao huffed, and he puffed, and he blew Shaq down"**

Signs held up by two fans among the 16,285-strong, sold-out Compaq Center crowd that came to watch Yao's first NBA encounter with Shaquille O'Neal.

Houston Chronicle, January 18, 2003

In an interview with ESPN's David Aldridge during the
2002 World Basketball Championship in Indianapolis in
September, Yao was asked what he thought it would be like
to square off against Shaquille O'Neal once he reached the
NBA. Yao commented, **"I think it will be one-sided in my matchup against Shaquille O'Neal. He is much better than I at this point. I think the NBA is a very good classroom for me. I think I will learn from defeat and from my setbacks and it will set a foundation for me to improve in the future."**

ESPN.com, September 3, 2002

Ten days before the start of his rookie season, Yao was asked about the prospect of playing against O'Neal, the 7-foot-1, 338-pound, perennial All-Star center for the LA Lakers. Yao said, **"Every problem has to be faced. That's going to be a very important game for me. I'm not going to be looking at it as a normal game. I'm going to look at it as a more important game."**

NBA.com, October 20, 2002

Shaq on Yao, before the Lakers' November 17 game against the Rockets, which Shaq sat out with a toe injury:

"Whenever you have a guy who comes in like that, you have to take it to him before he takes it to you. He has all the tools, can shoot, dribble — he can play. He's no slouch . . . I've seen some of his highlights. He shall be 'The Man' in a few years to come."

Orange County Register, January 11, 2003

After that November 17 Lakers-Rockets matchup in which Yao tallied 20 points and six rebounds on 9-for-9 shooting in just 23 minutes of play, the injury-grounded O'Neal said to Yao, **"You played pretty good, Yao Ming."** Yao humbly replied, **"That's because you weren't there."**

Agence France-Presse, November 19, 2002

When fan balloting for the 2003 NBA All-Star Game ended in early January 2003, Yao had been voted the starting center for the Western Conference All-Star squad, ahead of Shaquille O'Neal. Uncomfortable with the honor, Yao remarked, **"He's the best center in the game. Why can't he start and I come off the bench?"**

Sporting News, January 17, 2003

In advance of Yao's first game against Shaq on January 17, 2003, the self-deprecating Yao mused, **"Physically, I may still be needing a little bit. I think I may need a suit of armor."** He also quipped, **"He has a lot of meat on his elbows, so maybe it won't hurt as much."**

SI.com, January 17, 2003

During the January 17 game against the Shaq-led Lakers, Yao made his presence felt immediately, blocking O'Neal's first three shots of the game and sinking three of his first four shots. It was clear that the big man from Shanghai was respectful but not afraid of Shaq. Yao also forced a bad shot by Kobe Bryant at the end of regulation and helped seal the Rockets' 108-104 overtime victory with an authoritative, two-handed dunk with 10.2 seconds left. Yao finished the game with 10 points, 10 rebounds and 6 blocks, five of them against O'Neal. After the game, Yao said, **"How should I put it: We beat the Lakers today, but Shaq is still Shaq. He's like a truck."**

Of the experience of trying to defend against O'Neal, Yao added, **"It wore me out. I don't know how to describe it because I've never encountered somebody that strong before."**

Associated Press, January 17, 2003

After the January 17 meeting with Yao and the Rockets, Shaq said, "He's a classy guy. I was looking forward to playing him. He's a great player. It's another challenge for me."

Lakers coach Phil Jackson referred to Yao as "the difference in the ballgame."

Lakers guard Kobe Bryant, recently listed in *The Sporting News* as the second-best player in the NBA, after O'Neal, also offered words of respect: "I know what I thought. This guy is not intimidated at all. Some guys are just flat-out scared of Shaq. And he didn't seem to be that way."

People's Daily, January 19, 2003
Orange County Register, February 18, 2003

In the days leading up to the January 17 Rockets-Lakers matchup, Shaquille O'Neal came under intense fire in the media for two incidents in which he said to a reporter in a mock Chinese accent, "Tell Yao Ming, 'ching-chong-yang-wah-ah-soh,'" and, in June of last year, responded to a question about Yao Ming on FOX's *Best Damn Sports Show Period* with kung fu movie dialogue rendered in a mock Chinese accent and accompanied by mock kung fu moves. Yao's comments to the media upon being asked about Shaq's actions were reflective of his gracious and conciliatory nature. "There are a lot of difficulties in two different cultures understanding each other. Especially two very large countries. The world is getting smaller, and I think it's important to have a greater understanding of other cultures. I believe Shaquille O'Neal was joking, but I think that a lot of Asian people don't understand that kind of joke," said Yao. "Chinese is hard to learn. I had trouble with it when I was little," quipped Yao.

Extending an olive branch to Shaq in the midst of the
media firestorm caused by O'Neal's insensitive comments,
Yao invited Shaq to his Houston-area home for dinner while
Shaq was in town to play the Rockets on January 17.
O'Neal had to decline the invitation due to a prior
commitment with his daughter who lives in Houston.
Once again defusing a highly-charged situation with self-
deprecating humor, Yao mimicked a kind of relief at Shaq
not being able to make it for dinner, joking with reporters,

"I was worried there wouldn't be enough food in the refrigerator."

Newsday, February 9, 2003

Stung by media criticism of his misguided and
inappropriate attempt at humor, Shaq had planned to tell
Yao he was sorry in Mandarin before the tip-off. As the
game was about to start, Shaq embraced Yao and whispered
to him in English, "I love you, we're friends." Yao later
deadpanned, **"I thought of reminding him he just got married."**

ESPN The Magazine, February 3, 2003

{8}
Houston
Ham

Asked in a game against the Los Angeles Lakers whether he had noticed any of the numerous movie stars in attendance at the Staples Center, including Jack Nicholson, Yao said, **"No."**

A few minutes later, Yao picked up his sixth foul, fouling him out of the game. On the play, he made merely incidental contact with Lakers power forward Mark Madsen but Madsen flopped backwards as if he had been clobbered and Yao was called for an offensive foul. Yao was then asked whether he thought his sixth foul had been a good call. He replied, **"Like I said, there were a lot of movie stars here."**

San Francisco Chronicle, February 21, 2003

Upon arriving in Houston and being besieged by the media, the 7-foot-5 Yao asked reporters how they had managed to recognize him. **"You didn't know what I looked like,"** he deadpanned.

Chicago Tribune, January 26, 2003

On May 1, 2002, Yao Ming held a one-hour, pre-draft workout at Loyola University in Chicago for interested NBA teams. Representatives from 26 NBA teams and over 160 members of the media were on hand to see the big man from Shanghai first-hand. After the workout ended, reporters were handed the following written statement from Yao:

"I would like to express my sincere gratitude to all NBA teams for showing interest in me. I am honored by your presence. And I hope I have not disappointed you with my performance today. Proper credit is also due to the members of the media. The game of Cat 'n' Mouse is stressful, but your resourcefulness and work ethic are something I think we players should emulate. Journalism is a profession I respect a great deal. Just give me some more time to warm up. I look forward to taking each and every one of you to dinner sometime in the future. But the check is on you if your reporting makes me look bad."

Philadelphia Daily News, May 2, 2002

Since coming to America to play, Yao has consistently employed a light-hearted sense of humor to maintain his sanity in the face of relentless attention from the media.

Peering at a reporter's notebook recently, Yao joked,

"Some reporters in China, I think their notes look like English. Yours look like Chinese."

Newsday, February 9, 2003

Bearing in mind the well-known fact that he stocks his fridge at home with bottles of Starbucks Frappuccino, Yao was asked about his experience in Seattle when he was in town to play the Supersonics. "I'm disappointed," said Yao, smiling, "I thought there would be a Starbucks on the bench, being here in Seattle."

Seattle Times, November 30, 2002

As to why he had not yet dined at a Chinese restaurant in his new hometown of Houston, which has plenty of Chinese restaurants, Yao explained that it was because **"there's really good Chinese food at my house."**

USA Today, October 29, 2002

Asked about whether he has adjusted to the demands made upon him by the American media, Yao quipped, **"I dislike the traffic more than I dislike you."**

Yao had a chance to give the press another good-natured ribbing two months later when he said that his five favorite words in the English language were, **"This is the last question."**

Houston Chronicle, December 24, 2002
USA Today, February 28, 2003

After enduring 70 takes over the course of eight hours shooting what turned out to be an extremely well received Visa ad for the Super Bowl, Yao waxed philosophical about the silver lining to his grueling day: **"In basketball,"** said Yao, **"you don't have a chance to go back and do it again."**

USA Today, January 23, 2003

With his incredible height advantage over his opponents in the Chinese Basketball Association, Yao was asked why he did not score all of his points on layups and rim-rattling dunks, instead of the 18-foot jumpers he so often took. **"First of all, I'm not buff enough,"** he replied. **"I got pushed away from the basket. And even when I didn't, I couldn't get anyone to throw me a pass."**

When asked the logical follow-up question of why his teammates didn't, then, simply lob the ball to him closer to the basket, Yao intoned cheekily, **"You know that. But somebody doesn't know."**

Sports Illustrated, October 28, 2002

Lesley Visser, CBS Sports broadcaster, was in Shanghai to interview Yao Ming for HBO's *Real Sports with Bryant Gumbel*. During her time with Yao, Visser got a sneak peek at the light-hearted wit that the generally-reserved Shanghai native would soon be sharing with basketball fans in America. Visser recalls the following interaction: "He only spoke once to me in English. The rest was through a translator. I think he was making $80,000 for the Shanghai Sharks, and I said to him, 'You stand to earn great wealth. How do you think you'll handle it?' He said — and this was the only time he spoke English to me — 'I'll get used to it.'"

Houston Chronicle, June 27, 2002

On November 26, 2002, Yao and his teammates played the
Portland Blazers for the second time this season. Yao
struggled in his matchup with one of his boyhood idols,
Blazers center Arvydas Sabonis, who stands 7-foot-3 and is
listed at 292 pounds but looks to be considerably heavier.
Asked about getting his shot blocked by the beefy Sabonis,
Yao replied, **"I think I need to eat more,
because he's very strong."**

San Jose Mercury News, November 28, 2002

Asked what it was like growing up in Shanghai always being so much taller than the other children his age, Yao said, **"Well, I guess I had to pay the bus fare earlier than anyone else. And the doors seemed to be getting shorter for me."**

ESPN.com, September 3, 2002

When a reporter recently asked Yao why he was so tall, Yao shot back with a grin, **"Can you tell me why you're so small?"**

New York Post, February 25, 2003

Tony Ronzone, director of international scouting for the Detroit Pistons, made the trek to Shanghai in 1998 to check out Yao's on-court talent, but it was at a meal at Yao's home that Ronzone earned his keep for the Dallas Mavericks, his employer at the time. The scout was invited to dinner at Yao's family's one-bedroom, 12th-floor apartment on the prospect's 18th birthday. During dinner, though, Yao's mother served dishes so spicy that Ronzone perspired continuously as they ate. Said Ronzone, "Yao kept giving me a towel to wipe my head. He told me, 'You sweat more at the house than on the basketball court.'"

Oakland Tribune, June 2, 2002

Asked about meeting the Chicago Bulls' rotund general manager Jerry Krause prior to the 2002 NBA Draft, Yao said, laughing, **"He ate twice as much as I did."**

Chicago Sun-Times, January 27, 2003

Despite a more than respectable 10-point, 10-rebound, 6-block performance by Yao in his first game against Shaquille O'Neal on January 17, nothing in his five seasons in the Chinese Basketball Association had prepared the Rockets center for the singular experience of banging under the basket with the 7-foot-3-inch behemoth with the Superman tattoo. At his first opportunity to rest, Yao plopped his exhausted frame down on the bench between teammates Juaquin Hawkins and Bostjan Nachbar.

Said Yao, **"He's 350 pounds."** Hawkins replied, "That's all right, stay aggressive. Make him guard you." Yao: **"He's 350 pounds."**

In the locker room after the game, Yao attempted to describe Shaq to Team Yao, his small group of business and personal advisors. **"Like a meat wall,"** he said.

ESPN The Magazine, February 3, 2003

LA Lakers center Shaquille O'Neal sat out his much-anticipated second game against Yao Ming with a sore knee. Without the perennial All-Star to contend with under the basket, Yao had a big game, posting 24 points and 14 boards. Unfortunately, the Lakers' other superstar, Kobe Bryant, played lights-out, scoring 52 points in the double-overtime thriller. After the game, Yao joked about how he had anticipated having an easier time without Shaq's presence on the floor: **"I figured we could be a little more relaxed without him on the court. Maybe next time Kobe won't play."**

Associated Press, February 20, 2003

At home in Houston, Yao sleeps in a custom, nine-foot bed. On the road, however, he struggles to accommodate his 7'5" frame into even a king-size hotel bed. Michael Lu, the director of housekeeping at the Oakland Marriott City Center, where the Rockets stay when they are in town to play the Golden State Warriors, happened to read a story in a Chinese newspaper describing Yao's hotel bed woes. So in preparation for the Rockets' stay at the hotel for their November 27 game against the Warriors, Lu and his house-keeping staff engineered a 10-foot-long bed by attaching a roll-away to a king-size mattress. Yao slept so well on Lu's creation that he begged him in Chinese to **"hold that bed for me!"**

Sports Illustrated, February 10, 2003

Just minutes before his scheduled media session two days before the 2003 All-Star Game, Yao was in his Atlanta hotel room lamenting the fact that he would not be able to wear his brand new suit because the custom shoes that matched the suit had not arrived in time. Yao joked, **"They told me the shoes got stuck at U.S. Customs — they were made in Brazil. I thought the league is all-powerful, but I guess we don't own the U.S. Customs, even though my shoes are custom-made. My GQ moment is a missed opportunity."**

Houston Chronicle, February 9, 2003

Asked what he thought of the possibility that he might succeed Michael Jordan as basketball's biggest celebrity, Yao said, **"I hope the media will not start following me to the men's room."**

Newsday, February 9, 2003

During the frenzied 2003 All-Star Weekend press conference with Yao – only he and Michael Jordan, of all the NBA All-Stars, were the object of so much media interest as to warrant private news conferences – one reporter, overwhelmed by the electric atmosphere surrounding Yao's table, exclaimed, "This is bigger than Tiger [Woods] at the Masters." Yao remarked, **"A basketball is bigger than a golf ball."**

Milwaukee Journal Sentinel, February 8, 2003

Asked what he planned to do when he retires, Yao replied,
"I will probably join the mass media,
because I have always been bothered by
the mass media. And if I cannot beat
them, I will join them."

Baltimore Sun, February 9, 2003

{9}
It's a Ming Thing —
You Wouldn't
Understand

When Yao's number 15 jersey was retired by the Shanghai Sharks, his former team in the CBA, a grateful Yao took out a full-page ad in Shanghai's major newspaper to express his appreciation to his fans. In the ad, he invoked an old Chinese saying: **"How does a single blade of grass thank the sun?"**

Sporting News, January 17, 2003

Keith Jones, Houston Rockets director of player personnel and athletic trainer, on the Tao of Yao:

"He is wise beyond this league, the way he looks at life. A normal NBA guy's bubble is pretty limited. Someone found out they were a good athlete at 9-10 years old, they got circled in. But his life, his education in China and his culture, and now two cultures, his circle is just so big. He can combine a lot of little things in life, his view, things that people have never seen or have failed to see that way, and that's his sense of humor. He can make light of anything."

Associated Press, February 5, 2003

Asked what he had learned from the experience of being so famous in China, Yao said, **"Well, you have to be yourself. I try to still live my life and be myself and try not to be restricted by this cage thing fame brought with it."** When asked to elaborate on his "cage" reference, Yao added, **"I'm talking about specific examples. For example when I go shopping, there are a bunch of crowds surrounding me. And that makes me feel like I'm in a cage."**

ESPN.com, September 3, 2002

In discussing a December loss to the Los Angeles Clippers, perennial NBA basement-dwellers, Yao offered the following cryptic remark: **"Sometimes the hardest challenges are easier than the more difficult ones."**

Hartford Courant, January 25, 2003

Upon considering his experience thus far in the NBA, Yao said, "It is hard to pick out the one part that has been the hardest. I've had ups and downs like the waves of the ocean."

Boston Globe, February 24, 2003

Yao was asked whether his training in China had prepared him for the experience of playing in the NBA. He replied thoughtfully, **"Let me make a comparison: It's like a pen in two different persons' hands. It is used differently and it writes something differently, but it still has use and it still accomplishes something."**

Interpreter Colin Pine later added his own thoughts on Yao's words: "He likes to makes comparisons like that. When he likes the question and it's something he hasn't heard before, he likes to use that kind of imagery."

Canadian Press, March 5, 2003

Wistfully reflecting upon the significance of a botched dunk early in the season, Yao mused, **"When you have pitiful moments, that makes the good moments more valuable."**

Newsday, February 9, 2003

Asked about being named the Western Conference's
starting center for the 2003 NBA All-Star Game, Yao said,
"I am honored. I hope to play well in the
game. I think I might have to take a
sleeping pill before I can go to sleep
tonight. To have this rare opportunity is
a rare opportunity."

Atlanta Journal-Constitution, January 23, 2003

When he was asked how surprised he was to be leading Shaquille O'Neal in All-Star balloting, Yao gave a response that confused even his translator Colin Pine. **"My eyes seem to be bigger than my mouth, and my mouth seems to be bigger than a bicycle tire,"** said Yao. Pine later clarified that Yao was alluding to the wide-eyed, open-mouthed expression a person has when hearing something astonishing.

Toronto Star, January 12, 2003

Asked how difficult it was to learn the hook shot, Yao offered the following analogy: **"It's like if you had to get adjusted to using chopsticks to eat."**

Forth Worth Star-Telegram, February 2, 2003

After a loss to Dallas in which he posted breakout statistics, with 30 points and 16 rebounds, a contemplative Yao noted, "You have to understand, I play the game in two parts. One part is the enjoyment of playing. The other part is, of course, winning. Today, I achieved half of that."

Star Tribune, December 20, 2002

Asked in mid-November whether he had anything to say to his critics, many of whom had already dismissed him as a flop, Yao said, **"There's nothing I can really say,"** he said. **"Basketball is not something that you can talk about, it's an action through which you can show people. I just think I need to show them on the court."**

Associated Press, November 15, 2002

Asked in December — after the media had almost unanimously begun to sing his praises — if he had anything to say to those who had written him off, Yao said, "At first, when I wasn't playing well, I also wasn't satisfied."

Newsday, December 28, 2002

Demonstrating a keen awareness of the nature of media attention, Yao said, "There are only two ways how the media is talking about you — winner or loser. There is no other opinions in middle. Some players are content to be the blue-collar class of the league. I never dare to think about to be that type . . . There are always some reporters keep reminding me that 'there are billions of Chinese people watching you from behind.' I must set the goal to be one of the best, otherwise the Chinese fans will dump me. I'm trying to do my best on the first step here. After that I'll focus on the second and the third. To enjoy the life in a simply way. This is my life and it helps me a lot."

Xinhua News Agency, December 29, 2002

Yao was asked how he wanted to be remembered when his career was over. He replied, **"I don't know how to describe it exactly. But I hope through me, people will be more interested in basketball. This is a great sport to get into, to play and participate in. And this is what I want other people to remember, through me, to understand through me."**

ESPN.com, September 3, 2002

Yao's earliest experience with the sport of basketball was not exactly the stuff of All-Star dreams. When his third grade elementary school class was playing basketball in the gym, his teacher asked who could shoot the ball from the foul line. The unanimous reponse was, "Yao Ming." **"This made me very proud at that time, but one of my classmates did better than me, and this remained a sore point for some time,"** said Yao with a grin. **"Such was my first close contact with basketball."**

When Rockets coach Rudy Tomjanovich was trying to teach the team a particular zone defense, Yao jokingly suggested that the coach ought to consult his mother, who once played in a similar defense with the Chinese national women's team. Said Yao's mother, **"There is an expression in China. Bystanders sometimes see things more clearly than the person in the middle of the situation."**

Houston Chronicle, December 24, 2002

Commenting on the relentless demands on his time placed on him by press inquiries, promotional activities, photo shoots and other off-court commitments, Yao said, **"I am a basketball player, and I would like to focus my energy on basketball. The other things, I would rather not do. It is not something I am greatly interested in, but I know it is my responsibility."**

Yao's first U.S. television commercial featured the 7'5" Yao in an airplane sitting next to 2'8" Verne Troyer, who owes his celebrity status to the Austin Powers movies. Yao pulls out a 12-inch Apple PowerBook laptop computer but gets trumped by Troyer, who pulls out a 17-inch PowerBook, eliciting an envious chuckle from his much-bigger travel companion. Asked about his experience filming the commercial, Yao said, **"It was pretty funny. But the process of making it was very tiring. I had to sit there with lights on my face. It felt like I was right up against the sun."**

Sports Illustrated, January 27, 2003

Asked about how he felt when his Shanghai Sharks won the Chinese Basketball Association championship, Yao remarked, **"At the time, I thought about all the players that had come before me in Shanghai, who had the same goal for us, who had worked very hard for it, and we were only the lucky ones who were able to reap the fruit of their work."**

ESPN.com, September 3, 2002

Prior to making his professional debut for the Houston Rockets as the number one pick in the 2002 NBA Draft, Yao was asked about his NBA career goals. Said Yao, **"Apart from Iverson and Duncan, few No. 1 selected in the NBA drafts have given an outstanding performance. To improve my skills, I must set myself exacting targets. It doesn't matter whether I win the final championship or not. As long as I have tried my best, I will have no regrets."**

China Today, September 2002

After one game early in his rookie season in which he was hacked and roughed up repeatedly, Yao sat down on the Houston bench and noted stoically, **"That is not an honorable team."**

Sports Illustrated, January 27, 2003

Yao, on what he has learned from his Rockets teammates:

"A lot of things that when you're watching TV you don't see. Only when you're in the game, and on the court, do you really experience them and understand them. They've told me that when I'm on the court, I have to look at the game like it's a war, and I can't be a gentleman on the court."

World News Now on ABC, December 24, 2002

Yao's thoughts on having his jersey retired by the Shanghai Sharks: "There are a lot of athletes in the history of China that are qualified to have their numbers retired as well," said Yao. "So I feel fortunate to be the first. My father also wore the No. 15 when he played. I guess the only thing I feel sorry about is that my son might not be able to wear the number."

Chicago Sun-Times, December 31, 2002

On team versus individual accomplishments: "I feel I have only done my job if my team wins. That is my only goal." As an afterthought, Yao added, "I do have to learn more of the culture in the United States."

Memphis Commercial Appeal, December 13, 2002

Yao, two months into his first NBA season, after his stellar play began to cause a stir among sports fans and media: "I've kept telling myself to be aware of setbacks. What I have achieved now here could not be called success."

Xinhua News Agency, December 29, 2002

Nelson Luis, the Rockets' director of media relations, on Yao: "He's a very humble person. Very humble. He's the kind of guy who, really, if he could kind of be in obscurity, he would do it. Just go out and play basketball."

Alex Carcamo, former opponent of Yao Ming in the Chinese Basketball Association, on Yao: "When I found out he rides a bicycle to practice and that his dream was to own a car, I said, 'You should have 50 cars by now.' He's a humble person, intimidating on the floor but one of the nicest people off the floor."

Sacramento Bee, December 10, 2002
Philadelphia Daily News, May 30, 2002

Ric Bucher, senior writer for *ESPN The Magazine*, said,
"He's the most humble, unassuming superstar I've ever met . . . Yao looks at all this attention as a phenomenon, not some reflection of him being great."

The following story from Yao's past, as told by his childhood friend Zhu Jun Wei, supports this assessment: While an up-and-coming center in his mid-teens for the Shanghai junior team, Yao led the junior Sharks to a championship. As Zhu recalled, "Bonuses were paid to all the team members. The coach thought Yao Ming was great so he gave him an extra 20,000 yuan bonus [about $2,400] and Yao shared it with the others."

Times Herald-Record, February 25, 2003
New York Times, February 8, 2003